Amelia to Zora

Twenty-Six Women Who Changed the World

Cynthia Chin-Lee   Illustrated by Megan Halsey and Sean Addy

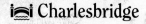 Charlesbridge

To my children, Vanessa and Joshua—C. C.

To the women who have changed MY world, the Dorothys, Nancy, Jodi, Sonya, Diane, Winky, Melanie, and Robin—M. H.

To my wife, Tonya, the most famous woman in my world. And to Megan, thanks.—S. A.

Text copyright © 2005 by Cynthia Chin-Lee
Illustrations copyright © 2005 by Megan Halsey and Sean Addy

Published by Charlesbridge
85 Main Street
Watertown, MA 02472
(617) 926-0329
www.charlesbridge.com

Library of Congress Cataloging-in-Publication Data
Chin-Lee, Cynthia.
   Amelia to Zora : twenty-six women who changed the world / Cynthia Chin-Lee ;
illustrated by Megan Halsey and Sean Addy.
    p. cm.
   ISBN 1-57091-522-9 (reinforced for library use)
1. Women—Biography—Juvenile literature. I. Halsey, Megan. II. Addy, Sean. III. Title.
CT3207.C49 2005
920.72—dc22   2004003847

Printed in Korea
(hc) 10 9 8 7 6 5 4 3

Illustrations done in mixed media
Display type set in Amigo and text type set in New Baskerville and Cataneo
Color separated, printed, and bound by Sung In Printing, South Korea
Production supervision by Brian G. Walker
Designed by Diane M. Earley

A is for Amelia, celebrated pilot and adventurer. When she was seven, Amelia Earhart, her sister, and a neighbor built a roller coaster. They made the tracks from fence rails propped on a toolshed roof and the cab from a wood packing box attached to roller skate wheels. Amelia took the first ride on the homemade coaster, which was so steep she somersaulted head-over-heels when the cab hit the ground. Later, at age 23, she was struck with flying fever after going to an air show. Amelia worked several jobs so she could afford flying lessons. On her 24th birthday Amelia bought her own plane.

Amelia set many records. She was the first woman to fly solo across the United States. She was the first person to fly alone from Hawaii to California. In 1937 the now-world-famous Amelia and her navigator attempted to fly around the world. They had made three-quarters of the almost 30,000-mile journey when they disappeared over the Pacific Ocean.

"Women must try to do things as men have tried. When they fail, their failure must be but a challenge to others."

Amelia Earhart (1897–1937)

FLIGHT PLANNING/PREPARA
3	MISSION PLANNING
BRIEFING
14	PREFLIGHT
15	PRETAKEOFF
16	TAKEOFF
DEPARTURE
17	CLIMB

B is for Babe, Olympic athlete extraordinaire. As a kid, Mildred Didrikson Zaharias earned the nickname "Babe," after baseball great Babe Ruth, because of all the softballs she whacked out of the park. From softball, she moved on to basketball, in which she helped her high school team gain the national championship. Babe won more medals and set more records than any athlete of her time, man or woman. She excelled in many different sports, including diving, tennis, track and field, and golf.

Babe won so many events in so many sports that when she entered the 1932 Olympics, she was allowed to participate in only three events. She won gold medals in javelin and the 80-meter hurdles. Babe was denied the gold medal in the high jump because the judges objected to her technique of hurling herself headfirst over the pole, now a standard practice. Later she took up golf and won 17 straight amateur tournaments, a record that still stands.

"It's not enough to just swing at the ball. You've got to loosen your girdle and really let her fly."

Babe Didrikson Zaharias (1914–1956)

5

C is for Cecilia, astronomer and the first

woman professor at Harvard University. Cecilia Payne-Gaposchkin was stargazing with her mother when she saw a meteor blaze across the sky. She decided then, at age five, to become an astronomer. After graduating from Cambridge University in England, she moved to the United States to find a job in astronomy research.

Cecilia worked at the Harvard observatory and received the first doctorate degree in astronomy that the university awarded. As a woman, she faced low wages and slow advancement, but her persistence, intelligence, and hard work were eventually rewarded. In 1956 Cecilia became the first woman professor at Harvard University as well as the first woman to be a department chair. Author of eight major books on astronomy, she called the stars her "friends."

"Do not undertake a scientific career in quest of fame or money. There are easier and better ways to reach them. Undertake it only if nothing else will satisfy you. . . ."

Cecilia Payne-Gaposchkin (1900–1980)

D is for Dolores, co-founder of the United Farm Workers (UFW). At age 14, Dolores Huerta helped her family by working an after-school job in the packing sheds of Stockton, California. The first in her family to attend college, Dolores left her job as a teacher because she felt she could help her students more by helping their parents, who were struggling farm workers.

Quick-witted and fiery, Dolores helped organize a strike of workers to protest low wages. If she found workers were ready to give up and go to work, she blocked their cars with her truck or hid their car keys to make sure the strike was successful. Along with Cesar Chavez, Dolores helped organize the UFW boycott against California growers of lettuce and table grapes. They protested the low pay and the unhealthy conditions that the farm workers faced at work. After the successful boycott, she negotiated the union's first contract with the growers. Beaten by union busters, arrested more than 20 times, Dolores also fights for the rights of women and all Latinos in the United States.

"Si, se puede!" (Yes, we can!)
Dolores Huerta (1930–)

E is for Eleanor, first lady and political leader. Born into a wealthy family, Anna Eleanor Roosevelt lived a privileged life, but she also faced many hardships. Both her parents died before she was 10, so Eleanor lived with her grandmother until she graduated from school. She did social work in New York City, helping poor immigrants and speaking up for workers' rights. During this time Eleanor became friends with her fifth cousin, Franklin Roosevelt, whom she later married. In 1933 Eleanor's husband was elected president. In her role as first lady, Eleanor fought for the rights of the poor on farms and in cities.

Eleanor had amazing energy at home and in her career. She raised five children, owned and taught at a private school for girls, ran emergency programs for the Red Cross, and visited U.S. soldiers all over the world. At age 61, Eleanor became the first U.S. representative to the United Nations, and she spent the rest of her life promoting peace.

"You gain strength, courage, and confidence by every experience in which you really stop to look fear in the face."

Eleanor Roosevelt (1884–1962)

F is for Frida, painter and folklorist. Frida Kahlo, Mexico's most famous woman artist, was a free-spirited and naughty child. She often got into trouble with her strict mother but was the favorite of her father, a photographer. When Frida was six, she was stricken with polio, which made her right leg stop growing. To strengthen herself, she played what were then considered boys' sports—soccer, wrestling, and boxing. At age 18, Frida was almost killed in a serious bus accident.

During her long recovery from this accident, Frida began to paint. She showed her paintings to Mexico's most famous painter, Diego Rivera. Later they were married. Both Frida's marriage and health had their ups and downs, but through her suffering she painted with humor and imagination. In addition to canvas, she painted on surfaces like copper, tin, and wood. She taught art to students in Mexico City, encouraging them to draw and paint everyday things such as jars, furniture, and toys.

"The only thing I know is that I paint because I need to, and I paint always whatever passes through my head, without any other consideration."

Frida Kahlo (1907–1954)

G is for Grace, inventor and computer pioneer. At age seven, curious Grace Hopper took apart several alarm clocks to figure out how they worked. Later she became the first woman to earn a doctorate degree in mathematics at Yale University. She helped make UNIVAC, the first all-purpose computer. Then she invented the first computer compiler, a program that translates words into codes that can be understood by computers. Grace co-created the computer language COBOL, one of the first computer languages used for business and still used today.

Grace popularized the term "computer bug" after her assistants found a moth stuck in a room-sized computer called the Mark I. They plucked the moth out and pasted it in a notebook, writing, "First actual case of a bug being found."

"Humans are allergic to change. They love to say, 'We've always done it that way.' I try to fight that. That's why I have a clock on my wall that runs counter-clockwise."

Grace Hopper (1906–1992)

10

H is for Helen, writer, speaker, and advocate for women and people with disabilities. When Helen Keller was six, a young teacher named Anne Sullivan came to teach her. Until then, the blind and deaf Helen threw wild tantrums to get her way, but thanks to Anne's loving persistence, Helen began to learn. First she learned sign language, and then she learned to read braille, which she mastered in five languages. Although public speaking terrified her, Helen overcame her fears so she could speak out for causes such as women's right to vote, just working conditions for the poor, and international peace.

With the help of her teacher, Anne, Helen was able to graduate with honors from Radcliffe College (part of Harvard University). She wrote several best-selling books, and championed the rights of women, the disabled, and minorities.

"I thank God for my handicaps, for through them,
I have found myself, my work, and my God."

Helen Keller (1880–1968)

I is for Imogen, photographer of people and plants. While in high school, Imogen Cunningham saw a show of Gertrude Kasebier's photos, which so enchanted her that she decided to become a photographer. Imogen's father built a darkroom in a woodshed for her. Then Imogen sent away for a camera and a how-to book and began photographing.

After college, Imogen worked in a photographer's studio and eventually opened her own portrait studio. Imogen loved taking pictures of people and felt that the key to making a portrait was understanding the person being photographed. Besides portrait photography, Imogen became famous for her plant photography. She turned to plants because, as a mother of three sons, she could photograph them quickly between chasing her boys. The forthright and funny Imogen spent more than 70 years in photography, working into her 90s.

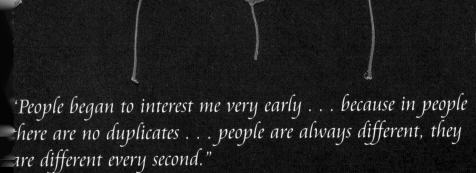

"People began to interest me very early . . . because in people there are no duplicates . . . people are always different, they are different every second."

Imogen Cunningham (1883–1976)

J is for Jane, chimpanzee expert and scientific naturalist. One night when Jane Goodall was little, her family couldn't find her and called the police. Jane had snuck into the farm's henhouse to watch the chickens. She said, "Where is the hole big enough for the eggs to come out?"

After reading stories about Africa, Jane dreamed of going there to live with wild animals. Years later she sailed to Africa and worked with anthropologist Louis Leakey. At his suggestion, Jane began her famous studies of chimpanzees. She watched a chimp, who poked a termite mound for food by using a twig. Her discovery that animals, and not just humans, could use tools changed the current thinking in animal studies. Not content to simply study and number her chimpanzees, Jane named each chimp and described their personalities and relationships.

"We have a choice to use the gift of our life to make the world a better place—or not to bother."

Jane Goodall (1934–)

K is for Kristi,

Olympic gold medalist and professional skater. Born with deformed feet, Kristi Yamaguchi had to wear corrective shoes and braces on her legs as a toddler. Attracted by the grace and beauty of ice-skating, six-year-old Kristi begged her parents for skating lessons. In her first competition she placed 12th out of 13. Undaunted, Kristi persuaded her parents of her commitment and continued her lessons, practicing three to four hours a day, six days a week.

In 1989, with pairs partner Rudy Galindo, Kristi won a gold medal in the National Pairs Skating competition. In 1991 she won the World Singles championship, and in 1992 she won the gold medal at the Winter Olympics. Now a professional skater, Kristi has started the Always Dream Foundation, which strives to make a positive difference in children's lives.

"When I'm skating, I feel like I can do anything. I feel like I can stay out there forever."

Kristi Yamaguchi (1971–)

L is for Lena, entertainer and civil rights activist. Lena Horne had a difficult childhood; her home life was unstable, so Lena often lived with relatives. At age 16, Lena started her own career, first as a dancer and then as a singer.

As a black singer she faced much racism. Lena performed for white audiences but was sometimes banned from staying in the same hotels as whites. Lena had the opportunity to work in Hollywood, so she moved from the East Coast to California. However, she couldn't get good parts and refused to take parts that portrayed blacks as menial. Throughout her life, Lena has supported the civil rights movement by donating time and money to groups that promote equal treatment for people of all races.

In her show business career, Lena spent most of her time entertaining in clubs and in concert. In 1981 she won a special Tony award for her show *Lena Horne: The Lady and Her Music.*

"You have to be taught to be second class; you're not born that way."

Lena Horne (1917–)

M is for Maya, architect and artist. Growing up, Maya Lin liked to stay home to study or make things. She made crafts with any material she could find—paper, string, and even scraps of silver. Her daily visits to her father's ceramic studio and her mother's poetry inspired Maya's art.

As a college student, Maya won a competition to create a memorial dedicated to the Vietnam War veterans. The memorial's stunning design launched Maya's architecture career. Since then she has designed monuments, homes, museums, and outdoor sculptures in a fresh and imaginative way.

"Somewhere between science and art, art and architecture, public and private, east and west . . . I am always trying to find a balance between these opposing forces, finding the place where opposites meet."

Maya Lin (1959–)

N is for Nawal,

medical doctor, writer, and fighter for women's rights. When Nawal El Sadaawi was born in Egypt, the births of boys were celebrated but the births of girls were mourned. Often, girls married as early as 10 years old and were expected to obey their husbands, who could punish them if they disobeyed. Nawal, however, fought the traditions of her society and became a medical doctor and writer.

Because of her honest portrayals of the life of Arab women, she was fired from her job and put in prison. Even in prison, Nawal continued to write and used a roll of toilet paper as her notepad. After her release from prison, Nawal received death threats and decided to leave her country. She taught in the United States and Europe. She has written 27 books about the treatment of women in the Arab world.

"Danger has been a part of my life ever since I picked up a pen and wrote. Nothing is more perilous than truth in a world that lies. . . . There is no power in the world that can strip my writings from me."

Nawal El Sadaawi (1931–)

O is for Oprah, talk-show host, actress, and entrepreneur. Oprah Winfrey was so smart that she asked her kindergarten teacher to move her to first grade; she also skipped second grade. Oprah's childhood was not easy, though. At different times she lived with her grandparents, her mother, and finally her father. She was abused as a child but found comfort in reading books about other people who overcame similar hardships.

Oprah won a scholarship to Tennessee State University and began working in radio and television. Her show *A.M. Chicago* became a hit and was renamed the *Oprah Winfrey Show*. Launched nationally in 1986, the show made Oprah a household name. Constantly seeking new challenges, she runs a film production company, acts in movies, and publishes a national magazine. Oprah's success has enabled her to do good work for others through her own charity, helping various causes around the world and encouraging volunteerism in others.

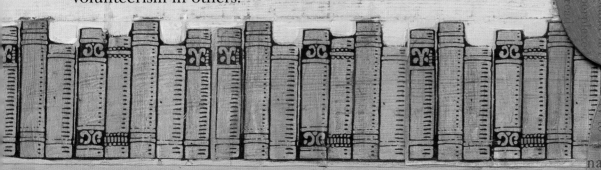

"Follow your instincts. That's where true wisdom manifests itself."

Oprah Winfrey (1954–)

P is for Patricia, champion of the family, congresswoman, and executive. When Patricia Schroeder was a child, her family moved around a lot. To make friends, she lined up her toys on the sidewalk and sat down next to them. The toys attracted kids and she made friends right away. That's why she says she is good at campaigning.

Pat worked her way through the University of Minnesota, graduated with honors, and went on to Harvard Law School. After she moved to Denver, Colorado, with her husband, Pat ran for Congress, not really expecting to win the election. She was the mother of two young children when she was elected. She went on to serve 12 terms as a congresswoman.

In Congress, she served on many important committees and championed laws to benefit women and families. After leaving Congress, Pat became president of the Association of American Publishers where she works to promote books and to preserve freedom of speech.

"Patriotism and courage are not exclusively masculine traits. . . . Women were a major force against slavery, for expanded political rights, for good government, and for governmental involvement with the poor and dispossessed."

Patricia Schroeder (1940–)

Q is for Quah Ah, Pueblo painter. When

Maria Antonia Peña was four, she was given the Native American name Quah Ah, meaning "little bead." Quah Ah, also called Tonita, was raised in the traditions of the Pueblos in New Mexico. When her mother died, she lived with her aunt, a potter, who taught her how to make pottery, a role usually reserved for men.

With a teacher's encouragement, Quah Ah and a group of artists painted Pueblo ceremonies and daily life. The only woman in this group, Quah Ah concentrated on painting women. In the 1930s she was asked to paint a series of murals for the Santa Fe Indian School, where she also taught art.

Despite her success in art, Quah Ah was criticized by both traditional Pueblo Indians, who thought she should stay at home, and by others who did not like her to paint Pueblo ceremonies that they considered secret. A trailblazer, Quah Ah is a role model for women and Native American artists.

"Painting-wise, there was only Tonita Peña. She was the rebellion way back then in the early 1920s. She gave me the inner strength that I needed to dare the men to put me in my own place or let me go."

Pablita Velarde, painter, speaking about Quah Ah

(also known as Tonita Peña)

Quah Ah (1893–1949)

R is for Rachel, mother of the environmental movement. As a young girl, Rachel Carson loved to explore the fields around her home. At age 10 she had her first story published in a children's magazine. She attended college to study literature, but she became interested in biology instead.

When she got a job writing radio scripts for the Bureau of Fisheries, she was able to combine her two favorite activities: writing and biology. Her writing was so moving that her boss encouraged her to send articles to magazines, and so Rachel began her writing career.

Rachel's book *The Sea Around Us* became a bestseller and won the National Book Award. In 1958 Rachel received a letter describing how a pesticide called DDT was killing songbirds. Rachel investigated the problem, writing a book about the dangers of pesticides. That book, *Silent Spring*, created an uproar, and DDT was banned in most of North America.

"Now, I truly believe that we in this generation must come to terms with nature, and I think we're challenged as mankind has never been challenged before to prove our maturity and our mastery, not of nature, but of ourselves."

Rachel Carson (1907–1964)

S is for Suu Kyi

(pronounced soo CHEE), fearless voice of Burma. At age two, Daw Aung San Suu Kyi lost her father, who had led Burma to independence from Great Britain. As a young girl, Suu Kyi was afraid of the dark. To conquer her fear, she walked around her home at night without turning on the lights.

When Suu Kyi grew up, she graduated from Oxford University in England, where she married and had two sons. She returned to Burma to care for her mother, who was dying. On her return, Suu Kyi found her country suffering from a poor economy and a harsh military government. She joined others to form a democratic party to oppose the ruling government.

Because of her support for democracy, Suu Kyi was arrested. Although she could have left Burma to rejoin her husband and sons in England, she believed she should not enjoy her own happiness when so many of her people were suffering. In 1991 Suu Kyi was awarded the Nobel Peace Prize for her dedication to peace and democracy in Burma. Because she was still under arrest, her sons accepted the prize.

Suu Kyi has been freed and imprisoned by her government many times. When she is not imprisoned, she is trying to set up a newspaper with the approval of her government.

"Values like love and compassion should be part of politics because justice must always be tempered by . . . compassion."

Daw Aung San Suu Kyi (1945–)

T is for Teresa, servant of the poor. At age seven, Teresa (or Agnes, as she was then called) lost her father; her mother raised Agnes and her siblings by selling cloth. Agnes loved the stories of the saints and of the missionaries who worked with the children of India. When she was 18, she embarked on a life as a nun, leaving her family in Yugoslavia and taking the name Teresa. After many years as a teacher and principal in India, Teresa felt that she received a calling from God to serve the poorest of the poor. She dreamed that no one should die before knowing God's love.

Teresa asked for permission from the Catholic Church to start her work. It took more than a year, but the Church finally approved her request. Her order, the Missionaries of Charity, has more than 3,000 members, with schools, soup kitchens, clinics, and homes for children with disabilities. In 1979 Mother Teresa received the Nobel Peace Prize.

"We are supposed to preach without preaching, not by words, but by our example, by our actions. All works of love are works of peace."
Mother Teresa (1910–1997)

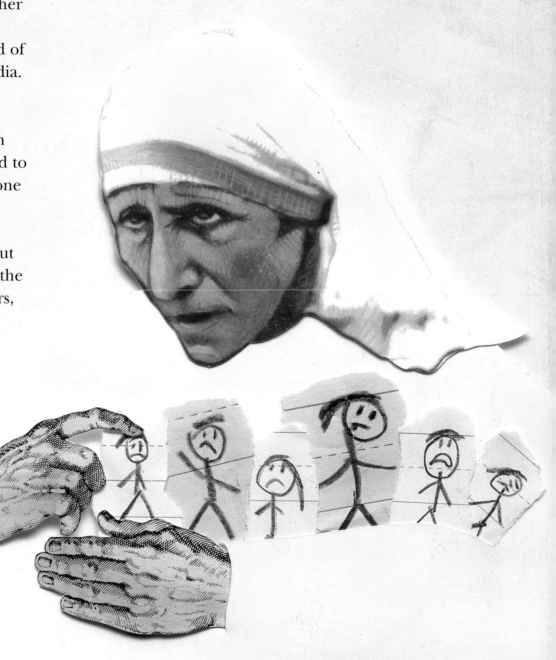

U is for Ursula, writer of poetry and prose. Daughter of a university professor and a writer, Ursula Kroeber Le Guin had a happy childhood full of music, books, and storytelling. As a teenager during World War II, she wandered the hills on her own while her brothers were in military service. Without television or other distractions, Ursula had time for thinking and soul-searching. Later she studied French and Italian literature at Radcliffe College and did graduate work at Columbia University. In addition to writing books, she taught French and creative writing.

Ursula writes many kinds of books, including fiction, fantasy, and books for children. Her best known fantasy works, the first four Earthsea books, have sold millions of copies, and her children's book *Catwings* is a favorite. Her books have won a National Book Award and many science fiction honors. Through her writings and in her life Ursula is active in speaking about civil and artistic rights.

"Language used as a means to get power or make money goes wrong: it lies. Language used as an end in itself, to sing a poem or tell a story, goes right, goes towards the truth."

Ursula K. Le Guin (1929–)

24

V is for Vijaya, freedom fighter, Indian diplomat, and first woman president of the United Nations. Daughter of Motilal Nehru, a nationalist leader, and sister of Jawaharlal Nehru, the first prime minister of free India, Vijaya Lakshmi Pandit studied at the University of Allahabad and abroad. Along with her family, she was a supporter of Mohandas (Mahatma) Gandhi and was arrested several times while fighting for India's independence from Great Britain.

Vijaya worked in local government and was elected to the legislature. She was the first Indian woman to hold a cabinet post and had a long career as a diplomat. She served as Indian High Commissioner to Great Britain and as ambassador to the Soviet Union, the United States, Mexico, the United Nations, Ireland, and Spain. In 1953 Vijaya became the first woman to be elected as president of the United Nations General Assembly.

"The more we sweat in peace, the less we bleed in war."

Vijaya Lakshmi Pandit (1900–1990)

W is for Wilma, a chief of the Cherokee Nation. When Wilma Pearl Mankiller was young, her family lived off the land by fishing, hunting, and gathering. When she was 10, a government agency convinced her parents to leave their home in Oklahoma and move to San Francisco to "work and live like white men."

In San Francisco, Wilma's classmates laughed at her name and made fun of the way she dressed. Wilma missed her home, but she settled into life in San Francisco, becoming active in the Native American community.

Still longing for her Cherokee home, Wilma returned to Oklahoma at age 32. She worked for the Cherokee Nation, the tribal government of the Cherokee tribe. Wilma ran for chief of the Cherokee Nation and won. In her two terms as chief, Wilma strengthened the financial foundation of the nation, supporting medical clinics, daycare centers, and environmental cleanup.

"I encourage young women to aspire to leadership. We are missing a lot of great solutions to society's problems because we do not hear women's voices in every sector of society."

Wilma Mankiller
(1945–)

X is for Xiefen

X is for Xiefen (pronounced she EH fun), founder of *Nubao* ("Women's Journal"). A year after her father started a newspaper in China, Chen Xiefen then 16 years old, set up her own paper. The monthly magazine supported women's education and rights and included essays, letters, speeches, and poetry.

A few years later Xiefen and her father, along with others, organized a girls' school. Xiefen set up another small school for women in the offices of her magazine. But in 1903 the Chinese government, disliking the antigovernment views of her father's paper and her magazine, closed down both publications. Xiefen and her family moved to Tokyo, Japan, and she published the fourth issue of her magazine there.

In Tokyo, Xiefen became chairperson of a group of patriotic Chinese women, and she also attended school. Xiefen's father tried to make her marry, but with her friends' support, she was able to refuse. Later she married a man of her own choice.

"There will be nothing women cannot study and no right that women cannot regain."

Chen Xiefen (1883–1923)

Y is for Yoshiko,

Y is for Yoshiko, elementary school teacher and author of more than 25 books for children. Born in the United States to parents from Japan, Yoshiko Uchida grew up with both Japanese and American traditions. As a young girl, she often didn't appreciate her Japanese heritage and didn't want to learn to read and write in Japanese, as her parents wished. She did like to write, though, and she made her first booklet about her dog, which had died.

During World War II, Yoshiko was imprisoned in an American internment camp in Topaz, Utah, along with her parents and sister. Eventually the government allowed her to leave to go to college. Later, during a visit to Japan, she studied and admired Japanese art and culture, which she has shared with others through her many children's books. In her books, Yoshiko wrote about the pride and self-esteem of Japanese Americans, which she did not find in books she had read as a child.

"*I had also discovered that writing in the booklet was a means, not only of holding on to the special magic of joyous moments, but of finding comfort and solace from pain as well. It was a means of creating a better ending than was possible in real life.*"

Yoshiko Uchida (1922–1992)

FLOWER
HANA
花

HOTDOG
HOTTO DOGG
ホットドッグ

HOUSE
IE
いえ

APPLE
RINGO
りんご

CAT
NEKO
ねこ

MY PET DOG
AIKEN

28

Z is for Zora, novelist, folklorist, and anthropologist. Sassy and proud, Zora Neale Hurston liked to do things her own way. As a little girl, she enjoyed making up stories, and her favorite place was the general store, where she listened to her neighbors swapping tall tales.

Zora's English teacher encouraged her writing, and she won a magazine story contest. In 1925 she moved to New York and won a scholarship to study anthropology. As an anthropologist, Zora traveled to the South and the Caribbean to collect the stories of African-Americans.

Zora wrote many articles and books. Other blacks criticized her for her viewpoints on race and for writing folklore, which some thought stereotyped them. Undaunted, Zora wrote true to her own beliefs and is widely admired for her writings.

"I know that nothing is destructible: things merely change forms. . . . Why fear? The stuff of my being is matter, ever changing, ever moving, but never lost."

Zora Neale Hurston
(1891–1960)

Selected Bibliography
(alphabetical according to subject)

Butler, Susan. *East to the Dawn: The Life of Amelia Earhart*. Reading, MA: Addison-Wesley, 1997.

Szabo, Corrine. *Sky Pioneer: A Photobiography of Amelia Earhart*. Washington, DC: National Geographic Society, 1997.

Johnson, William Oscar. *Whatta-gal: The Babe Didrikson Story*. Boston: Little, Brown, 1977.

Zaharias, Babe Didrikson. *This Life I've Led: My Autobiography*. New York: Barnes, 1955.

Gaposchkin, Cecelia Helena. *Cecilia Paine-Gaposchkin: An Autobiography and Other Recollections*. Katherine Haramundanis, editor. New York: Cambridge University Press, 1984.

Herrera, Hayden. *Frida: A Biography of Frida Kahlo*. New York: Harper & Row, 1983.

Whitelaw, Nancy. *Grace Hopper: Programming Pioneer*. New York: Scientific American Books for Young Readers, 1995.

Cunningham, Imogen. *Imogen Cunningham: Portraiture*. Text by Richard Lorenz. Boston: Little Brown, 1997.

Dater, Judy. *Imogen Cunningham: A Portrait*. Boston: New York Graphic Society, 1979.

Goodall, Jane. *My Life with the Chimpanzees*. New York: Pocket Books, 1996.

Lin, Maya. *Boundaries*. New York: Simon and Schuster, 2000.

Saadawi, Nawal. *A Daughter of Isis: The Autobiography of Nawal El Saadawi*: translated from the Arabic by Sherif Hetata. Distributed in the United States by St. Martins Press. New York: Zed Books, 1999.

Lowe, Janet. *Oprah Winfrey Speaks: Insight from the World's Most Influential Voice*. New York: Wiley, 1998.

Schroeder, Pat, with Andrea Camp and Robyn Lipner. *Champion of the Great American Family*. New York: Random House, 1989.

Gray, Samuel L. *Tonita Peña: Quah Ah, 1893–1949*. Albuquerque, NM: Avanyu Publishing, 1990.

Carson, Rachel. *Silent Spring*. Boston: Houghton Mifflin, 1962.

Ransom, Candice F. *Listening to Crickets: A Story About Rachel Carson*. Minneapolis, MN: Carolrhoda Books, 1993.

Aung San Suu Kyi. *Freedom from Fear and Other Writings*. Michael Aris, editor. New York: Viking, 1991.

Stewart, Whitney. *Aung San Suu Kyi: Fearless Voice of Burma*. Minneapolis, MN: Lerner Publications Company, 1997.

Pandit, Vijaya Lakshmi. *The Scope of Happiness: A Personal Memoir*. New York: Crown Publishers, 1979.

Simon, Charnon. *Wilma Mankiller: Chief of the Cherokee*. Chicago: Children's Press, 1991.

Mankiller, Wilma and Wallis, Michael. *Mankiller: A Chief and Her People*. New York: St. Martin's Griffin, 1999.

Lee, Lily Xiao Hong; Stefanowska, A. D.; and Wing-chung Ho, Clara, editors. *Biographical Dictionary of Chinese Women: The Qing Period*. New York: M. E. Sharpe, 1998.

Uchida, Yoshiko. *Desert Exile: The Uprooting of a Japanese American Family*. Seattle: University of Washington Press, 1982.

Uchida, Yoshiko. *The Invisible Thread: A Memoir*. Englewood Cliffs, NJ: J. Messner, 1991.

Hurston, Zora Neale. *Their Eyes Were Watching God*. New York: Perennial Classics, 1998.

Lyons, Mary E. *Sorrow's Kitchen: Life and Folklore of Zora Neale Hurston*. New York: Collier Books, 1993.

Author's Note

As a child I loved reading biographies. When my teachers assigned a book report, I'd head straight for the biography shelves at Murch Elementary School library in Washington, D.C. Reading people's life stories inspired me. I could empathize with their struggles, glory in their achievements, and use their examples to overcome the obstacles in my life.

Writing *Amelia to Zora* allowed me to do one of my favorite things—curl up with biographies of women I admire. Through each woman's experiences I lived vicariously and was transformed by her strength, courage, and determination. As you learn about these women I hope you will also see the possibilities in your own life.

I wanted the women I chose to be easy to identify with, so I looked for contemporary figures who were diverse in nationality, profession, race, and religion. Although each profile is short, my intent is to spark an interest and encourage further study of each woman. With so many women to choose from, it was hard to know where to start. I picked some famous women, but I wanted to highlight others who might be new to you.

I chose given names, rather than family names, for each woman, so that "A is for Amelia" instead of "E is for Earhart." Family names are usually based on a father's or husband's name. Using a woman's given name felt more personal to me. I followed this strategy with Asian names, in which the given name comes after the family name. Thus for Chen Xiefen, "X is for Xiefen." For Daw Aung San Suu Kyi, "S is for Suu Kyi." In Burmese, Daw is an honorary title, meaning aunt, Aung San is the family name and Suu Kyi is the given name.

As you get to know these women, I hope you will think of them as I do—kindred spirits whose words and actions will inspire and guide you.

Acknowledgments

The author thanks the following people for their support and help: Merry Banks, Dennise Brown, Nancy and William Chin-Lee, Peter Ching, Terri de la Peña, Debbie Duncan, Carole Eittreim, Nancy Farmer, Kenji Igarashi, Debbie Keller, Julia Lin, SuAnn and Kevin Kiser, Nina Ollikainen, Mimi Tam, Harold Underdown, and Monica Wong.